About the Book

Elma Gonzalez and her family were migrant farm workers. Elma had to leave school every spring to pick crops in the fields and did not return to school until late in the fall. Never giving up, she completed her education and went on to become an eminent scientist in charge of her own laboratory at the University of California, Los Angeles.

The story of Elma Gonzalez tells of a girl who triumphed over difficulties and achieved her goals by meeting life's challenges "one step at a time."

an American Women in Science biography

Scientist with Determination,
Elma Gonzalez

by Mary Ellen Verheyden-Hilliard

drawings by Marian Menzel

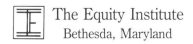

The Equity Institute

Bethesda, Maryland

This work was developed under a grant from the Women's Educational Equity Act Program, U.S. Department of Education. However, the content does not necessarily reflect the position of that Agency and no official endorsement of these materials should be inferred.

Library of Congress Cataloging in Publication Data

Verheyden-Hilliard, Mary Ellen.
   Scientist with determination, Elma Gonzalez.

   (An American women in science biography)
   Summary: A brief biography of the Mexican-American woman who grew up in a family of migrant workers and went on to earn a doctorate in cellular biology and eventually head her own research laboratory.

   1. Gonzalez, Elma—Juvenile literature. 2. Women cytologists—United States—Biography—Juvenile literature. 3. Cytologists—United States —Biography—Juvenile literature. [1. Gonzalez, Elma. 2. Scientists] I. Menzel, Marian, ill. II. Title. III. Series: Verheyden-Hilliard, Mary Ellen. American women in science biography.
   QH31.G58V47   1985   574.87'092'4 [B][92]   84-25981
   ISBN 0-932469-01-9

Scientist with Determination,
Elma Gonzalez

"Elma. Time to go to work."
Mrs. Gonzalez spoke softly to the
sleeping Elma.

Twelve-year-old Elma kept her
eyes shut. She did not want to go
to work. She wanted to go to
school.

Every spring Elma left school.
She traveled from job to job with
her family. They picked fruits

and vegetables for the big landowners. Then, in October, Elma returned to school. Elma and her family were migrant farm workers. "Migrant" means "traveling."

Picking was hard, hot work. It made Elma's back hurt. Worse, it kept her from school. But Elma knew that the money the family earned in the spring and summer paid for food and clothes in the winter.

One step at a time, Elma thought. First, I help earn the money. Then, I go to school. I can do it if I try.

Elma opened her eyes and got out of bed. She got dressed for the long day in the fields.

Elma Gonzalez was born in Mexico on June 6, 1942. Her father and mother brought her to America when she was six years old. The family settled in Texas. They worked for a rancher. They lived in a cabin on his ranch.

"In America you will go to school," Elma's father told her. "Education is a way out of being poor."

"I am going to school," Elma told everyone. But something happened. The school would not send a bus all the way to the ranch to pick up just one child.

Elma's parents had no way to get her back and forth to school in the city. Elma could not go to school after all!

Elma's father had a very old geography book. Elma loved that book. It told her about the world beyond the ranch. She asked questions about the pictures in the book.

"Why are there mountains in some countries? Why do different animals live in different countries?" No one she knew could answer all her questions.

"Someday, I'll find the answers to my questions," she said to herself. Her dream kept her going when things were hard.

Mr. and Mrs. Gonzalez knew how much school meant to Elma. So they let her go to the city to live with an older cousin. There she could start school. But the cousin did not like the way Elma acted.

"Girls should not ask so many questions," her cousin said. Elma was sent back to the ranch.

Back home, Elma's father helped her learn about numbers. He taught her how to add and subtract. But that was not enough for a girl with so many questions in her head.

Every year her parents asked
the school to send the bus. Every
year the school refused.

Three years passed.

Elma was nine years old. She had never been to school. She sat on the fence by the road. She wondered if the bus would ever come.

One evening Elma was out by the road. Her father called. "Good news, Elma. I found a new home for us in the city."

"Do I go to school?" Elma held her breath for the answer.

"Yes," her father said. "You go to school."

When Elma started school, she did not speak English very well. She asked all her questions in Spanish. The teacher also spoke Spanish, but that did not help.

"You ask too many questions," her teacher said.

Elma did not understand. What was wrong with wanting to learn?

After school, Elma sometimes listened to a radio quiz show where children answered the questions. The questions were about history, science, and math. The show was called "The Quiz Kids." Elma liked listening to the questions and learning the answers.

Sometimes Elma and her mother listened to the radio together. They listened while Elma's mother sewed. She sewed beautifully. She made dresses for Elma to wear to school.

"I'll call you 'our lawyer,' I think." Her mother smiled. "You are so interested in questions and answers!"

Elma's mother was proud of her daughter. She wanted her to learn as much as she could.

In junior high school, school finally became the wonderful place Elma always hoped it would be. The teachers liked girls and boys to ask questions. Elma found a friend who liked to read as much as she did. Her friend's name was Margaret.

Margaret and Elma had library cards. They went to the library two or three times every week to get new books to read.

Elma and Margaret liked math too. They asked the principal if they could take algebra. The

algebra class was fun. Elma liked
solving the algebra puzzles.

In high school Elma played on the girls' basketball team. One year her team won 17 games and lost only two games! Elma joined the science club. She was elected to the student council.

Elma and Margaret began to talk about college. Margaret's family could pay for college. Elma and her family were still poor. Elma still picked fruit in the spring and summer to earn money for the winter.

"If someone would just lend me the money for college, I know I could get a good job after college and pay back what I owe," Elma said. She decided to talk to her father.

"Do you remember, Papa, when you told me that education is a way out of being poor?"

Her father nodded his head.

"Well, I get good grades. I can get a student loan to pay for college if you will help me. With a college education, I can help us all."

At first her father did not like the idea. If the loan was not paid back, the whole family would be in debt. Elma's mother and father talked about the loan. Finally, they decided. Elma could take out a student loan. The Gonzalez family would stand behind her.

Elma studied science in college. She thought she would be a teacher. Her college professor had another idea.

"Elma, you would be a good research scientist. We all know," he said with a smile, "how much you like to ask questions and look for answers! That's what research scientists do—ask questions about the world we live in. Then they use math and science to find the answers."

Imagine, Elma thought, I would be paid to do what I like to do! What could be better than that?

Elma went to Rutgers University. She studied cellular biology, the science of how cells live and grow. She earned a doctorate, the highest degree a scientist can earn. She repaid her student loans. She became a research scientist.

Now Dr. Elma Gonzalez works in her laboratory studying the cells of which all living things are made. One of the ways she does this is by studying the castor bean seed. She breaks the seed open and takes out a piece of the center. She breaks the cells in this small piece of seed with a sharp blade. She places the broken cells in a centrifuge.

The centrifuge is a powerful machine. It spins the small pieces from inside the cell so fast that they separate from each other. Dr. Gonzalez wants to know about the proteins inside the cell. Do they have to be in a special place to do their job? If they are in the wrong place, does that cause disease? What Dr. Gonzalez learns helps scientists understand how human cells work—how diseases in human cells may cause blindness, deafness, or other problems.

Elma's laboratory is at the University of California in Los Angeles. She likes being a research scientist. She likes teaching students at the university. She likes trying to help young students become scientists. She *never* tells her students that they ask too many questions!

Sometimes, when a student is discouraged, Elma shares what she figured out when she was a little girl:

"Don't give up," Dr. Elma Gonzalez says. "Just take it one step at a time. It may be hard, but you can do it if you try!"